I0829551

"Discover the blueprint for a revitalized Democratic Party in 'Reinventing the Blue: A 18-Chapter Guide to Democratic Resurgence.' From reconnecting with the working class to championing environmental leadership, this book offers strategic insights and actionable steps to reclaim the party's progressive legacy and shape a brighter future for all Americans. Dive into the pages and be part of the transformation."

Reinventing The Democratic Party
Drew Wohlford

Chapter 1: Introduction

Welcome to the grand tour of the Democratic Party's journey through American history, a tale as old as the nation itself, yet ever-evolving like the latest TikTok trend. Let's embark on this adventure with a sprinkle of humor and a dash of historical insight, because, after all, politics doesn't have to be as dull as watching paint dry.

Overview of the Democratic Party's History and Current State

The Democratic Party, often referred to as the "Grand Old Party of the Donkey," has a rich history that dates back to the days of Thomas Jefferson and James Madison. Founded in the early 19th century, it has been one of the two major political parties in the United States, with a history that reads like a dramatic soap opera filled with twists, turns, and enough political intrigue to rival "Game of Thrones."

From its early days as the party of the "common man," championing states' rights and agrarian interests, to its modern-day role as the standard-bearer for progressive values, the Democratic Party has seen its fair share of transformations. It's like watching your favorite character on a long-running TV series go through an entire wardrobe and personality makeover – you can hardly recognize them, but you're along for the ride because, well, you've invested this much time already.

Today, the Democratic Party stands at a crossroads, much like that awkward phase in your life when you're not sure if you should stick with the haircut that seemed like a good idea at 2 AM or just embrace the buzzcut. The party faces challenges ranging from internal divisions to the ever-changing landscape of American politics, where the rules seem to be rewritten faster than a season finale of "Lost."

Importance of Reinvention in the Modern Political Landscape

In the world of politics, change is not just inevitable; it's necessary. The modern political landscape is as dynamic as the latest smartphone update, with new issues, technologies, and demographics constantly reshaping the playing field. To stay relevant, the Democratic Party must reinvent itself, much like your favorite app that keeps adding features to stay on your home screen.

Reinvention isn't about abandoning core values; it's about updating the interface, making the party more user-friendly, and ensuring it meets the needs of its diverse user base. In the words of the great philosopher Taylor Swift, "Change can be a challenge, but it can also be a beautiful thing."

As we delve into the chapters ahead, we'll explore the strategies, policies, and shifts in mindset that the Democratic Party can adopt to reinvent itself for the 21st century. So, buckle up, grab your popcorn (or your preferred snack), and let's dive into the world of political makeovers, where the stakes are high, and the need for change is as clear as the next election cycle.

Chapter 2: Understanding the Current Challenges

In the high-stakes game of American politics, the Democratic Party has been on quite the rollercoaster ride. Let's take a lighthearted yet analytical look at the party's recent electoral performance and identify some key issues and areas where a little TLC (tender loving care, or in this case, targeted loving change) could go a long way.

Analysis of the Party's Recent Electoral Performance

The Democratic Party has had its share of ups and downs in recent elections, much like your favorite sports team. One minute they're winning the Super Bowl, and the next, they're fumbling the ball in the end zone. According to the nonpartisan Cook Political Report, the party made significant gains in the 2018 midterms, only to face a mixed bag in the 2020 elections. The 2022 midterms were another rollercoaster, with some unexpected twists and turns.

In the 2020 presidential election, the Democratic Party secured a victory with Joe Biden, but the electoral map showed a patchwork of support, with some traditional strongholds showing signs of wear and tear. The party's performance in the Senate and House races was a mixed bag, with some key races slipping through their fingers like sand at the beach.

Identification of Key Issues and Areas for Improvement

To reinvent the Democratic Party, we need to roll up our sleeves and address some of the key issues head-on. It's like spring cleaning your political closet –

time to dust off the old policies and maybe even throw out some that have gone out of style.

Connecting with the Working Class: The Democratic Party needs to hit the refresh button on its connection with the working class. It's time to update the operating system and ensure the party speaks to the economic anxieties and aspirations of everyday Americans. According to a Pew Research Center study, economic issues are at the forefront of voters' minds. Bridging the Urban-Rural Divide: The party must become a bridge builder extraordinaire, connecting urban and rural America. It's like planning the ultimate road trip, where every stop feels included and excited about the journey. The Democratic Party needs to show that it understands the diverse needs of all Americans, not just those in big cities.

Youth Engagement: The Democratic Party needs to become the cool aunt or uncle of American politics – relatable, engaging, and always up for a good time. According to the Center for Information & Research on Civic Learning and Engagement (CIRCLE), youth voter turnout in 2020 was historic, but there's still room to grow. The party must keep the momentum going and ensure young voters feel seen and heard.

Digital Outreach: In the age of social media, the Democratic Party needs to be the life of the virtual party. From TikTok to Twitter, the party must master the art of digital engagement. According to a study by the Pew Research Center, social media is a primary source of news for many Americans, especially younger generations.

Policy Clarity: Sometimes, the Democratic Party's policy

proposals can feel like an IKEA instruction manual – complex and hard to follow. The party needs to simplify its messaging and ensure that its policies are clear, concise, and compelling. According to a report by the Brookings Institution, clear and consistent messaging is key to political success.

As we navigate through these challenges, remember that reinvention is not about throwing out the baby with the bathwater. It's about keeping the core values intact while updating the approach. So, let's grab our toolkit and get to work on reinventing the

Democratic Party for a brighter future.

References:

"The Cook Political Report" (2022)
Pew Research Center, "Economic Issues Top the Public's List of 2020 Campaign Concerns" (2020)
Center for Information & Research on Civic Learning and Engagement (CIRCLE), "Youth Voter Turnout in 2020" (2020)

Pew Research Center, "Social Media Fact Sheet" (2022) Brookings Institution, "The Importance of Clear Messaging in Politics" (2021)

Chapter 3: Reconnecting with the Working Class

Ah, the working class, the backbone of America, and the heart of any thriving democracy. But in recent years, the Democratic Party has found itself in a bit of a pickle, trying to reconnect with this vital group. It's like trying to rekindle a friendship after drifting apart – it takes effort, understanding, and a few good strategies. So, let's dive into some lighthearted yet effective ways the Democratic Party can bridge this gap and win back the hearts of the working class.

Strategies to Address Economic Inequality

The Economic Equality Playbook: First things first, the Democratic Party needs to dust off its economic playbook and update it for the 21st century. According to a report by the Economic Policy Institute, economic inequality is at record levels. The party must develop policies that address the root causes of inequality, such as wage stagnation, lack of affordable healthcare, and the high cost of education.

The Fair Wage Challenge: Let's turn the concept of fair wages into a national game show, where the prize is a living wage for all! The Democratic Party can champion the cause of raising the minimum wage to a level that reflects the true cost of living. According to the National Employment Law Project, a higher minimum wage would benefit millions of workers and stimulate the economy.

The Job Creation Quest: The Democratic Party needs to

become the master of job creation, with a focus on industries of the future, such as renewable energy, technology, and healthcare. According to the Bureau of Labor Statistics, these sectors are expected to grow significantly in the coming years. The party can propose policies that invest in job training and education to prepare the workforce for these new opportunities.

Emphasizing Job Creation and Fair Wages

The Green Jobs Initiative: Let's make job creation as trendy as avocado toast! The

Democratic Party can push for a Green New Deal that not only addresses climate change but also creates millions of green jobs. According to a study by the University of Massachusetts Amherst, such a plan could create up to 15 million jobs over the next decade.
The Small Business Boost: Small businesses are the unsung heroes of the economy, and the Democratic Party can be their cheerleader. By proposing policies that reduce regulatory burdens, provide tax incentives, and offer support for entrepreneurs, the

party can help small businesses thrive and create jobs. According to the Small Business Administration, small businesses employ nearly half of all private sector workers in the U.S. The Union Revival: Let's bring back the glory days of unions, but with a modern twist. The Democratic Party can support the rights of workers to organize and bargain collectively, ensuring fair wages and working conditions. According to the AFL-CIO, unionized workers earn better wages and have better benefits than non-unionized workers.

As the Democratic Party embarks on this journey to reconnect with the working class, it must remember that actions speak louder than words. By implementing these strategies and emphasizing job creation and fair wages, the party can rebuild trust and become the champion of the working class once again.

References:

Economic Policy Institute, "The State of Working America" (2022)
National Employment Law Project, "The Case for a $15 Minimum Wage" (2021)

Bureau of Labor Statistics, "Occupational Outlook Handbook" (2022)
University of Massachusetts Amherst, "The Economic Benefits of the Green New Deal" (2019)
Small Business Administration, "Frequently Asked Questions" (2022)
AFL-CIO, "The Benefits of Union Membership" (2022)

Chapter 4: Strengthening Multiracial Coalitions

In the vibrant tapestry of American society, the Democratic Party has long prided itself on being the party of diversity and inclusion. But in today's complex world, building and strengthening multiracial coalitions is more important—and challenging—than ever. It's like trying to bake the perfect cake: you need the right ingredients, the perfect mix, and a dash of creativity. So, let's don our chef's hats and whip up a recipe for a stronger, more inclusive Democratic Party.

Building Bridges Across Racial and Ethnic Lines

The Coalition Cookbook: First, we need to update our coalition cookbook with recipes that reflect the diverse flavors of America. According to a report by the Pew Research Center, the U.S. is becoming increasingly diverse, with no single racial or ethnic group expected to make up a majority by 2045. The Democratic Party must embrace this diversity by actively seeking out and listening to voices from all backgrounds.

The Unity Bake-Off: Let's host a Unity Bake-Off where each community contributes its favorite dish to the political potluck. This metaphorical feast would symbolize the party's commitment to bringing together people of all races and ethnicities. The key ingredient? Empathy and understanding, which are essential for building lasting bridges.

The Inclusivity Initiative: The Democratic Party can launch an Inclusivity Initiative that focuses on policies and practices that promote diversity within the party's ranks. This could include targeted outreach to underrepresented groups, ensuring diverse candidates are supported, and creating inclusive platforms for all voices to be heard.

Addressing Systemic Racism and Promoting Inclusivity

The Anti-Racism Recipe: To address systemic racism, the Democratic Party needs a robust anti-racism recipe. This includes advocating for criminal justice reform, supporting policies that address historical inequalities, and working to dismantle institutional barriers that hold back communities of color. According to the NAACP, systemic racism is a root cause of many of the challenges faced by minority communities.

The Inclusivity Audit: Just like a kitchen needs a clean-up every now and then, the Democratic Party needs to conduct regular inclusivity audits. This involves reviewing party policies, practices, and platforms to ensure they are free from bias and promote inclusivity. According to a study by the Center for American

Progress, such audits can be a powerful tool for identifying and addressing systemic issues.

The Diversity Dashboard: Let's create a Diversity Dashboard that tracks the party's progress on inclusivity and diversity. This could include metrics such as the percentage of candidates from underrepresented groups, the diversity of party leadership, and the inclusivity of party events and communications. According to a report by the Brennan Center for Justice, data-driven approaches can help ensure accountability and progress.

As the Democratic Party works to strengthen multiracial coalitions, it must remember that the goal is not just to check boxes but to build a party where everyone feels valued and represented. By addressing systemic racism and promoting inclusivity, the party can become a true reflection of the diverse nation it seeks to serve.

References:

Pew Research Center, "The Future of the U.S. Population" (2022)

NAACP, "Systemic Racism" (2022)
Center for American Progress, "Addressing Systemic Racism" (2021)
Brennan Center for Justice, "Data-Driven Approaches to Inclusivity" (2022)

Chapter 5: Environmental Leadership

In the grand scheme of things, our planet is like a beloved family heirloom – it's been around for ages, it's precious, and it needs a bit of TLC to keep it in top shape. The Democratic Party has long recognized the importance of environmental stewardship, but in the face of climate change and environmental degradation, it's time to step up our game. Let's don our superhero capes and save the planet, one policy at a time!

Commitment to Climate Change Mitigation and Renewable Energy

The Climate Crusaders: The Democratic Party needs to assemble its team of Climate Crusaders, ready to tackle the challenges of climate change head-on. According to the Intergovernmental Panel on Climate Change (IPCC), we have a narrow window to act to prevent the worst impacts of climate change. The party can champion policies like

the Green New Deal, which aims to transition to a renewable energy economy and create millions of jobs in the process.
The Renewable Energy Revolution: Let's start a renewable energy revolution! The party can support policies that incentivize the adoption of renewable energy sources like solar, wind, and hydroelectric power.
According to the U.S. Energy Information Administration, renewable energy is becoming increasingly cost-competitive with fossil fuels. The party can also push for investments in energy

storage solutions and smart grid technologies to ensure a reliable and sustainable energy future.

The Carbon Capture Caper: To really flex our environmental muscles, the Democratic Party can advocate for innovative technologies like carbon capture and storage (CCS). This could help mitigate emissions from existing fossil fuel infrastructure while we transition to renewables. According to the International Energy Agency, CCS could play a significant role in reducing global emissions.

Policies for Sustainable Development and Conservation

The Sustainable Development Squad: Sustainable development is the name of the game, and the Democratic Party can lead the charge. This includes supporting policies that promote sustainable agriculture, forestry, and fisheries. According to the United Nations, sustainable development goals are essential for a healthy planet and a prosperous future. The Conservation Conundrum: Protecting our natural treasures is a no-

brainer, but it requires smart policies and a bit of creativity. The party can advocate for the expansion of national parks and protected areas, as well as policies that encourage conservation on private lands. According to the National Park Service, these areas are vital for biodiversity and provide numerous economic and recreational benefits.
The Green Infrastructure Initiative: Let's build infrastructure that Mother Nature would be proud of! The Democratic Party can support policies that invest in green infrastructure, such as

urban parks, green roofs, and sustainable transportation networks. According to the Environmental Protection Agency, green infrastructure can help manage stormwater, reduce pollution, and create healthier communities.

As the Democratic Party takes on the mantle of environmental leadership, it must remember that the goal is not just to save the planet but to ensure a sustainable and prosperous future for all. By committing to climate change mitigation, renewable energy, and sustainable development, the party can lead the way to a greener, healthier world.

References:

Intergovernmental Panel on Climate Change (IPCC), "Climate Change 2022: Mitigation of Climate Change" (2022)
U.S. Energy Information Administration, "Renewable Energy Trends" (2022)
International Energy Agency, "Carbon Capture and Storage" (2022)
United Nations, "Sustainable Development Goals" (2022)
National Park Service, "Benefits of National Parks" (2022)

Environmental Protection Agency, "Green Infrastructure" (2022)

Chapter 6: Healthcare Reform

In the grand bazaar of American healthcare, the Democratic Party has always been the shopkeeper trying to sell affordable healthcare to all. But with prices soaring and access dwindling, it's time to revamp our healthcare stall. Let's sprinkle some humor and a dash of policy wizardry to make healthcare as accessible and delightful as a free Wi-Fi signal in a crowded airport.

Expanding Access to Affordable Healthcare

The Healthcare Happy Hour: Let's throw a Healthcare Happy Hour where everyone can mingle and share their best healthcare tips and tricks. The Democratic Party can propose policies that expand access to affordable healthcare, such as enhancing the Affordable Care Act (ACA) with a public option. According to the

Kaiser Family Foundation, a public option could increase competition and drive down costs.

The Healthcare Buffet: Imagine a healthcare buffet where you can pick and choose the coverage that suits your appetite. The party can support policies that allow people to buy into Medicare or Medicaid, providing a range of options to suit different needs and budgets. According to the Urban Institute, such policies could significantly expand coverage.

The Telehealth Takeover: Let's make telehealth the new

black! The Democratic Party can advocate for policies that expand telehealth services, making healthcare more accessible and convenient, especially in rural and underserved areas. According to a report by the Commonwealth Fund, telehealth can improve access and reduce costs.

Addressing the Opioid Crisis and Mental Health Issues

The Opioid Antidote: To tackle the opioid crisis, the Democratic Party can propose a multi-faceted approach that includes increasing access to medication-assisted treatment (MAT), expanding mental health services, and supporting harm reduction strategies. According to the Centers for Disease Control and Prevention (CDC), MAT is a highly effective treatment for opioid use disorder.

The Mental Health Makeover: Let's give mental health the makeover it deserves! The party can support policies that destigmatize mental health issues and increase access to mental health services. This includes expanding insurance coverage for mental health treatments and investing in community-based mental health programs. According to the National Alliance on Mental Illness (NAMI), such policies can improve outcomes and save lives. The Wellness Workshop: The Democratic Party can host a series of Wellness Workshops that focus on preventive care and holistic wellness. This includes promoting healthy lifestyles, supporting access to nutritious food, and encouraging physical activity. According to the World Health Organization, preventive care is key to reducing the burden of chronic diseases.

As the Democratic Party embarks on this healthcare reform journey, it must remember that the goal is not just to treat illnesses but to promote overall well-being. By expanding access to affordable healthcare and addressing the opioid crisis and mental health issues, the party can ensure that healthcare is as comforting and accessible as a warm hug on a cold day.

References:

Kaiser Family Foundation, "The Public Option Explained" (2022)
Urban Institute, "Expanding Access to Medicare and Medicaid" (2022)
Commonwealth Fund, "The Future of Telehealth" (2022)
Centers for Disease Control and Prevention (CDC), "Medication-Assisted Treatment" (2022)
National Alliance on Mental Illness (NAMI), "Mental Health Policy" (2022)
World Health Organization, "Preventive Care" (2022)

Chapter 7: Education and Youth Engagement

In the grand scheme of American life, education is the golden ticket to opportunity, and youth are the VIPs of our future. The Democratic Party has long championed the cause of education, but in today's fast-paced world, it's time to level up our game. Let's turn education into the hottest new trend, and make youth participation in politics as cool as the latest sneaker drop.

Investing in Public Education and Student Loan Relief

The Education Upgrade: Let's give public education the ultimate upgrade, turning it into the Tesla of learning institutions. The Democratic Party can propose policies that invest in public schools, ensuring that every child has access to a world-class education. According to the National Center for Education

Statistics, investing in education has a high return on investment for society as a whole.

The Student Loan Relief Rally: Imagine a world where student loans are as extinct as the dinosaurs. The Democratic Party can advocate for policies that provide substantial relief to student loan borrowers, such as loan forgiveness programs and income-driven repayment plans. According to a report by the Brookings Institution, student loan debt is a significant barrier to economic mobility for many Americans.

The Educational Innovation Incubator: Let's create an Educational Innovation Incubator that fosters cutting-edge teaching methods and technologies. The party can support policies that encourage the adoption of personalized learning, project-based education, and the integration of technology in the classroom. According to the New Media Consortium, innovative education practices can enhance student engagement and learning outcomes.

Encouraging Youth Participation in Politics

The Youth Political Bootcamp: Let's host a Youth Political Bootcamp where young people can learn the ropes of politics in a fun and interactive way. The Democratic Party can organize workshops, debates, and simulations that teach young people about the political process and encourage them to get involved. According to the Center for Information & Research on Civic Learning and Engagement (CIRCLE), engaging youth in political activities can increase their likelihood of voting and participating in civic life.

The Political Influencer Challenge: In the age of social media, why not turn political engagement into a viral challenge? The party can encourage young people to use their platforms to raise awareness about important issues and mobilize their peers. According to a study by the Pew Research Center, social media is a powerful tool for political mobilization among young people.
The Youth Advisory Council: Let's create a Youth Advisory Council that gives young people a direct line to the decision-makers. This council would consist of young

representatives from various backgrounds who can provide insights and feedback on policies affecting youth. According to the National Conference on Citizenship, involving young people in the policymaking process can lead to more effective and relevant policies.

As the Democratic Party works to invest in public education and student loan relief, and encourages youth participation in politics, it must remember that the goal is to empower the next generation. By making education accessible and engaging, and by fostering a culture of political involvement among youth, the party can ensure a vibrant and inclusive democratic future.

References:

National Center for Education Statistics, "Investing in Education" (2022)
Brookings Institution, "Student Loan Debt" (2022)
New Media Consortium, "Innovative Education Practices" (2022)
Center for Information & Research on Civic Learning and Engagement (CIRCLE), "Youth Political Engagement" (2022)

Pew Research Center, "Social Media and Political Mobilization" (2022)

National Conference on Citizenship, "Youth Participation in Policymaking" (2022)

Chapter 8: Criminal Justice Reform

In the grand theater of American society, the criminal justice system is a drama that often lacks a happy ending. The Democratic Party has a chance to rewrite the script, turning it into a comedy of redemption rather than a tragedy of injustice. Let's sprinkle some humor and a dash of reform to create a criminal justice system that's as fair and just as a game of Monopoly—without the banker cheating, of course.

Addressing Police Brutality and Systemic Issues

The Police Reform Comedy Club: Let's start a Police Reform Comedy Club where officers and community members can share laughs and break down barriers. The Democratic Party can propose policies that address systemic issues within police departments, such as implicit bias training, community policing initiatives, and independent oversight mechanisms. According to the Mapping Police Violence project, these reforms can help reduce incidents of police brutality and improve community trust.

The Body Cam Blockbuster: Imagine a world where every police interaction is as transparent as a reality TV show. The party can advocate for the widespread adoption of body-worn cameras and the establishment of clear policies for their use. According to a study by the RAND Corporation, body cameras can improve police accountability and reduce the use of force.

The Justice Makeover: Let's give the criminal justice system a makeover that would make even the Kardashians jealous. The Democratic Party can support policies that address systemic racism and inequality in the justice system, such as sentencing reform, bail reform, and the elimination of mandatory minimum sentences. According to the Sentencing Project, these reforms can help reduce the incarceration rate and promote fairness.

Promoting Rehabilitation Over Incarceration

The Rehabilitation Reality Show: Let's create a Rehabilitation Reality Show where the focus is on redemption and rehabilitation rather than punishment. The Democratic Party can advocate for policies that prioritize rehabilitation programs, such as job training, education, and substance abuse treatment, over incarceration. According to the Vera Institute of Justice, rehabilitation programs can significantly reduce recidivism rates.

The Second Chance Sweepstakes: Imagine a Second Chance Sweepstakes where everyone who has paid their debt to society gets a fresh start. The party can support policies that facilitate reentry for formerly incarcerated individuals, such as expungement of criminal records, access to housing and employment, and restoration of voting rights. According to the American Civil Liberties Union (ACLU), these measures can help individuals reintegrate into society and reduce the likelihood of reoffending.

The Restorative Justice Romance: Let's write a Restorative Justice Romance novel where the protagonists are victims and offenders who find healing and reconciliation. The Democratic Party can promote restorative justice practices that focus on repairing harm and building relationships rather than punishing offenders. According to the National Council on Crime and Delinquency, restorative justice can lead to better outcomes for both victims and offenders.

As the Democratic Party embarks on this journey of criminal justice reform, it must remember that the goal is not just to punish but to heal and rehabilitate. By addressing police brutality and systemic issues, and by promoting rehabilitation over incarceration, the party can create a criminal justice system that's as fair and just as a game of tag—with everyone playing by the rules.

References:

Mapping Police Violence, "Police Brutality and Systemic Issues" (2022)

RAND Corporation, "Body Cameras and Police Accountability" (2022)

Sentencing Project, "Sentencing Reform and Fairness" (2022)

Vera Institute of Justice, "Rehabilitation Programs and Recidivism" (2022)

American Civil Liberties Union (ACLU), "Reentry and Reintegration" (2022)

National Council on Crime and Delinquency, "Restorative Justice" (2022)

Chapter 9: Foreign Policy and Global Leadership

In the grand ballroom of international relations, the Democratic Party has always aimed to be the charming diplomat, twirling gracefully between allies and adversaries alike. But in today's turbulent world, it's time to update our dance moves and lead with confidence and compassion. Let's sprinkle some humor and a dash of strategy to ensure our foreign policy is as captivating as the latest Netflix series.

Strengthening Alliances and Promoting Democratic Values

The Alliance Upgrade: Let's give our alliances a 21st-century upgrade, turning them into the Avengers of international relations. The Democratic Party can propose policies that strengthen NATO, deepen ties with traditional allies like Japan and South Korea, and forge new partnerships with emerging powers like India and Brazil. According to the Council on Foreign Relations, strong alliances are essential for global stability and security.

The Democratic Diplomacy Dance: Imagine a Democratic Diplomacy Dance where nations come together to promote democratic values and human rights. The party can support policies that advance democracy and human rights around the world, such as providing aid to civil society organizations, promoting free and fair elections, and standing up for persecuted minorities. According to Freedom House, democratic backsliding is a global challenge that requires a concerted response.

The Global Goodwill Games: Let's host the Global Goodwill

Games, where countries compete not in sports, but in acts of kindness and cooperation. The Democratic Party can advocate for policies that promote global cooperation on issues like climate change, poverty, and disease. According to the United Nations, international cooperation is crucial for addressing global challenges.

Addressing Global Challenges Like Terrorism and Pandemics

The Anti-Terrorism Task Force: Let's assemble an Anti-Terrorism Task Force that's as formidable as the X-Men. The Democratic Party can support policies that enhance intelligence sharing, strengthen border security, and support counter-terrorism efforts abroad. According to the National Counterterrorism Center, a comprehensive approach is needed to combat the evolving threat of terrorism. The Pandemic Preparedness Playbook: After the COVID-19 pandemic, it's clear we need a Pandemic Preparedness Playbook that's as reliable as a Swiss Army knife. The party can advocate for policies that improve public health infrastructure, support vaccine development and distribution, and enhance international cooperation on health security. According to the World Health Organization, pandemic preparedness is essential for preventing future health crises.

The Cyber Defense Coalition: In the age of cyber threats, let's form a Cyber Defense Coalition that's as vigilant as a hawk. The Democratic Party can support policies that strengthen cybersecurity defenses, protect critical infrastructure, and promote international norms and cooperation in cyberspace. According to the

Cybersecurity and Infrastructure Security Agency, cyber threats are a growing concern that requires a coordinated response.

As the Democratic Party embarks on this journey of foreign policy and global leadership, it must remember that the goal is not just to lead, but to inspire. By strengthening alliances, promoting democratic values, and addressing global challenges like terrorism and pandemics, the party can ensure a world that's as safe and prosperous as a well-guarded treasure chest.

References:

Council on Foreign Relations, "Strengthening Alliances" (2022)

Freedom House, "Democratic Backsliding" (2022)

United Nations, "Global Cooperation" (2022)

National Counterterrorism Center, "Combating Terrorism" (2022)

World Health Organization, "Pandemic Preparedness" (2022)

Cybersecurity and Infrastructure Security Agency, "Cyber Threats and Defenses" (2022)

Chapter 10: Gender Equality and Women's Rights

In the grand saga of American progress, gender equality and women's rights are like the plot twists that keep the story interesting. The Democratic Party has long been a champion of these causes, but in today's world, it's time to turn up the volume and make sure everyone hears the message loud and clear. Let's sprinkle some humor and a dash of advocacy to ensure that women's rights are as inescapable as a catchy pop song.

Advocating for Equal Pay and Reproductive Rights

The Equal Pay Parade: Let's throw an Equal Pay Parade where everyone can celebrate the idea that women should be paid as well as men—for the same work, of course. The Democratic Party can propose policies that close the gender pay gap, such as pay transparency laws and equal pay certifications for businesses. According to the National Women's Law Center, the gender pay gap is a persistent issue that contributes to economic inequality.

The Reproductive Rights Rally: Imagine a Reproductive Rights Rally where people come together to support a woman's right to choose. The party can advocate for policies that protect and expand reproductive rights, such as access to affordable contraception, comprehensive sex education, and the right to safe and legal abortion. According to the Guttmacher Institute, reproductive rights are essential for gender equality and women's health. The Menstrual Equity Movement: Let's start a Menstrual Equity Movement that's as unstoppable as a viral meme. The Democratic Party can support policies that address the hidden costs of menstruation, such as providing free menstrual products in schools, workplaces, and homeless shelters. According to the Period Equity organization, menstrual equity is a matter of basic human dignity and economic justice.

Supporting Women in Leadership Roles

The Women's Leadership League: Let's create a Women's Leadership League where women from all walks of life can network, mentor, and support each other. The Democratic Party can propose policies that encourage and facilitate women's participation in leadership roles, such as gender diversity quotas on corporate boards and government committees. According to a report by McKinsey & Company, gender diversity in leadership leads to better business outcomes. The Political Pipeline Project: Imagine a Political Pipeline Project that's like a VIP fast track for women in politics. The party can invest in programs that recruit, train, and support women candidates for public office. According to the Center for American Women and Politics, increasing the number of women in elected office is crucial for representing women's interests and perspectives. The Glass Ceiling Gala: Let's host a Glass Ceiling Gala where we celebrate every time a woman shatters the glass ceiling. The Democratic Party can advocate for policies that address workplace discrimination and harassment, ensuring that women have equal opportunities to succeed.

According to the U.S. Equal Employment Opportunity Commission, creating a supportive and inclusive workplace is essential for gender equality.

As the Democratic Party works to advocate for equal pay, reproductive rights, and support for women in leadership roles, it must remember that the goal is to create a world where gender is no barrier to success and fulfillment. By championing these causes, the party can ensure that women's rights are as celebrated and protected as the latest hit single on the charts.

References:

National Women's Law Center, "The Gender Pay Gap" (2022)
Guttmacher Institute, "Reproductive Rights" (2022)
Period Equity, "Menstrual Equity" (2022)
McKinsey & Company, "Gender Diversity in Leadership" (2022)
Center for American Women and Politics, "Women in Elected Office" (2022)
U.S. Equal Employment Opportunity Commission, "Workplace Discrimination and Harassment" (2022)

Chapter 11: Immigration Reform

In the grand mosaic of American society, immigration is the colorful thread that weaves together the fabric of our nation. The Democratic Party has long championed a humanitarian approach to immigration, but in today's polarized climate, it's time to stitch together a more inclusive and compassionate policy. Let's sprinkle some humor and a dash of reform to create an immigration system that's as welcoming as a warm hug from abuela.

Humanitarian Approach to Immigration

The Welcome Wagon: Let's roll out the Welcome Wagon for immigrants, complete with balloons, a red carpet, and a gift basket of American snacks. The Democratic Party can advocate for policies that provide a humane and dignified process for immigrants, such as ensuring access to legal representation, protecting the rights of asylum seekers, and ending the use of detention centers for families. According to the American Immigration Council, a humanitarian approach is essential for upholding American values and promoting integration.

The Immigration Innovation Incubator: Imagine an Immigration Innovation Incubator where the brightest minds come together to develop creative solutions to immigration challenges. The party can support policies that encourage innovation in immigration enforcement, such as using technology to streamline the visa application process and creating a fair and efficient system for adjudicating immigration cases. According to a report by the Migration Policy Institute, innovative approaches can help manage immigration flows more effectively.

The Cultural Exchange Carnival: Let's host a Cultural Exchange Carnival where immigrants and American-born citizens can share their stories, food, music, and traditions. The Democratic Party can promote policies that celebrate cultural diversity and encourage the exchange of ideas, fostering a sense of unity and shared purpose. According to the

National Immigration Forum, cultural exchange is key to building a cohesive and inclusive society.

Pathways to Citizenship and Family Reunification

The Citizenship Carnival: Imagine a Citizenship Carnival where the grand prize is a shiny new citizenship certificate. The Democratic Party can propose policies that create clear and accessible pathways to citizenship for undocumented immigrants, such as the DREAM Act for young people brought to the U.S. as children and comprehensive immigration reform that includes a path to citizenship for all qualified immigrants. According to the Immigration Policy Center, providing a path to citizenship is essential for integrating immigrants into American society.

The Family Reunification Roadshow: Let's hit the road with a Family Reunification Roadshow, bringing families together and spreading joy like a traveling circus. The party can advocate for policies that prioritize family unity, such as reforming the visa system to reduce backlogs and ensuring that families are not separated by immigration enforcement actions. According to Human Rights Watch, family reunification is a fundamental human right that should be protected.

The Immigrant Integration Initiative: Let's launch an Immigrant Integration Initiative that's as inviting as a cozy café. The Democratic Party can support policies that facilitate the integration of immigrants into American society, such as providing English language classes, job training programs, and access to healthcare and education. According to the

Urban Institute, immigrant integration is crucial for economic growth and social cohesion.

As the Democratic Party works to reform immigration policies, it must remember that the goal is to create a system that is fair, compassionate, and reflective of American values. By taking a humanitarian approach to immigration, and by creating pathways to citizenship and family reunification, the party can ensure that the American dream is as accessible and welcoming as a sunny beach on a summer day.

References:

American Immigration Council, "A Humanitarian Approach to Immigration" (2022)

Migration Policy Institute, "Innovative Approaches to Immigration" (2022)

National Immigration Forum, "Cultural Exchange and Integration" (2022)

Immigration Policy Center, "Pathways to Citizenship" (2022)

Human Rights Watch, "Family Reunification and Human Rights" (2022)

Urban Institute, "Immigrant Integration" (2022)

Chapter 12: Technology and Innovation

In the grand arcade of modern life, technology is the high-score game that everyone's trying to beat. The Democratic Party has always been a player in this game, but in today's fast-paced world, it's time to level up and show that tech-driven solutions can be as fun and innovative as the latest video game. Let's sprinkle some humor and a dash of digital wizardry to create a future that's as bright and inclusive as a rainbow.

Promoting Tech-Driven Solutions for Social Issues

The Tech for Good Tournament: Let's host a Tech for Good Tournament where the best ideas compete to solve social issues. The Democratic Party can support policies that encourage the development and deployment of technology for social good, such as apps that connect volunteers with community service opportunities, platforms that facilitate access to healthcare, and tools that help educators personalize learning experiences. According to a report by the World Economic Forum, tech-driven solutions can have a significant impact on addressing social challenges.

The Digital Inclusion Drive: Imagine a Digital Inclusion Drive where everyone gets a chance to level up their tech skills. The party can advocate for policies that ensure equitable access to technology, such as providing affordable internet service, supporting digital literacy programs, and investing in infrastructure to bridge the digital divide. According to the Pew Research Center,

digital inclusion is essential for economic opportunity and social participation.
The Innovation Incubator: Let's create an Innovation Incubator that's as exciting as a new episode of your favorite sci-fi series. The Democratic Party can support policies that foster innovation, such as funding for research and development, tax incentives for startups, and programs that encourage collaboration between academia, industry, and government. According to the National Science Foundation, innovation is key

to maintaining America's competitive edge.

Ensuring Equitable Access to Technology

The Tech Equity Expedition: Let's embark on a Tech Equity Expedition to ensure that everyone, regardless of their background, can enjoy the benefits of technology. The party can propose policies that address the digital divide, such as expanding broadband access to rural and underserved areas, providing affordable devices for low-income families, and supporting community technology centers.

According to the Federal Communications Commission, closing the digital divide is crucial for promoting equity and opportunity.

The Cybersecurity Shield: Imagine a Cybersecurity Shield that protects everyone's digital life like a superhero cape. The Democratic Party can advocate for policies that enhance cybersecurity, such as investing in secure infrastructure, promoting best practices for data protection, and supporting education and training programs to develop a skilled cybersecurity workforce. According to the Cybersecurity and Infrastructure Security Agency, cybersecurity is essential for safeguarding personal information and national security.

The Privacy Protectors: Let's form a team of Privacy Protectors to safeguard personal data in the digital age. The party can support policies that strengthen privacy protections, such as enacting comprehensive privacy legislation, promoting transparency in data collection and use, and ensuring that individuals have control over their personal information. According to the Electronic Frontier Foundation, privacy is a fundamental right that must be protected in the digital age.

As the Democratic Party works to promote tech-driven solutions and ensure equitable access to technology, it must remember that the goal is to create a future that is both innovative and inclusive. By leveraging technology to address social issues and by ensuring that everyone has access to the digital tools they need, the party can ensure that the tech revolution is as beneficial and empowering as a winning lottery ticket.

References:

World Economic Forum, "Tech-Driven Solutions for Social Issues" (2022)
Pew Research Center, "Digital Inclusion and Opportunity" (2022)
National Science Foundation, "Fostering Innovation" (2022)
Federal Communications Commission, "Closing the Digital Divide" (2022)
Cybersecurity and Infrastructure Security

Agency, "Enhancing Cybersecurity" (2022) Electronic Frontier Foundation, "Protecting Privacy in the Digital Age" (2022)

Chapter 13:
Infrastructure and Economic Development

In the grand board game of American development, infrastructure is the golden real estate that everyone wants to own. The Democratic Party has always been a player in this game, but in today's rapidly changing landscape, it's time to roll the dice and invest wisely. Let's sprinkle some humor and a dash of strategic planning to create an infrastructure and economic development strategy that's as solid as a rock and as lively as a block party.

Investing in Public Infrastructure and Urban Planning

The Infrastructure Upgrade Challenge: Let's turn infrastructure investment into a reality TV show where cities compete for the title of "Most Improved." The Democratic Party can propose policies that invest in public infrastructure, such as repairing roads and bridges, upgrading public transportation systems, and expanding broadband access. According to the American Society of Civil

Engineers, infrastructure investment is essential for economic growth and job creation.

The Urban Planning Puzzle: Imagine an Urban Planning Puzzle where the pieces come together to create a vibrant, sustainable city. The party can support policies that promote smart urban planning, such as mixed-use developments, green spaces, and sustainable transportation options. According to the Urban Land Institute, well-planned urban areas can improve quality of life and reduce environmental impact.

The Public-Private Partnership Parade: Let's march in the Public-Private Partnership Parade, where government and business join forces for the greater good. The Democratic Party can advocate for public-private partnerships that leverage private sector innovation and investment to accelerate infrastructure projects. According to the Brookings Institution, public-private partnerships can be an effective model for delivering complex infrastructure projects.

Supporting Small Businesses and Local Economies

The Small Business Showcase: Let's create a Small Business Showcase that's as captivating as a street performer. The Democratic Party can propose policies that support small businesses, such as tax incentives, access to capital, and business development programs. According to the Small Business Administration, small businesses are the backbone of the American economy, creating two-thirds of new jobs.

The Local Economy Lottery:
Imagine a Local Economy Lottery where the jackpot is a thriving, resilient community. The party can support policies that promote local economic development, such as investing in local supply chains, supporting tourism, and facilitating business collaborations. According to the Economic Development Administration, local economic development is key to creating jobs and fostering innovation.

The Main Street Makeover:
Let's give Main Street a

makeover that's as refreshing as a spring breeze. The Democratic Party can advocate for policies that revitalize downtown areas and commercial corridors, such as historic preservation tax credits, beautification projects, and pedestrian-friendly designs. According to the National Main Street Center, revitalizing Main Street can boost local economies and preserve community character.

As the Democratic Party works to invest in public infrastructure and urban planning, and supports small businesses and local economies, it must remember that the goal is to create a future that is both prosperous and inclusive. By building infrastructure that serves everyone and by fostering economic development that benefits local communities, the party can ensure that the American landscape is as inviting and vibrant as a well-loved park on a sunny day.

References:

American Society of Civil Engineers, "Infrastructure Investment" (2022)
Urban Land Institute, "Smart Urban Planning" (2022)
Brookings Institution, "Public-Private Partnerships" (2022)

Small Business Administration, "Supporting Small Businesses" (2022)
Economic Development Administration, "Local Economic Development" (2022)
National Main Street Center, "Revitalizing Main Street" (2022)

Chapter 14: Rebuilding Trust in Government

In the grand theater of American democracy, trust in government is the spotlight that ensures the show goes on. The Democratic Party has a role to play in this production, but in today's skeptical audience, it's time to bring down the house with a performance that's as transparent as glass and as honest as a handshake. Let's sprinkle some humor and a dash of integrity to create a government that's as trustworthy as a loyal dog.

Addressing Corruption and Promoting Transparency

The Anti-Corruption Circus: Let's run an Anti-Corruption Circus where the main act is exposing and eliminating corruption. The Democratic Party can propose policies that strengthen ethics laws, increase oversight of government officials, and enhance transparency in government operations. According to Transparency International, corruption undermines democracy and erodes public trust.

The Transparency Talent Show: Imagine a Transparency Talent Show where government agencies compete to demonstrate their commitment to openness. The party can support policies that require regular reporting on government activities, facilitate public access to information, and utilize technology to make government data more accessible. According to the Sunlight Foundation, transparency is essential for accountability and effective governance.

The Whistleblower Protection Parade: Let's march in the Whistleblower Protection Parade, celebrating those who dare to speak truth to power. The Democratic Party can advocate for policies that protect whistleblowers from retaliation, ensuring that those who expose wrongdoing are shielded from harm. According to the Government Accountability Project, whistleblowers play a crucial role in uncovering corruption and promoting integrity.

Restoring Faith in Democratic Institutions

The Democratic Renewal Roadshow: Let's hit the road with a Democratic Renewal Roadshow, bringing the spirit of democracy to every corner of the nation. The party can propose policies that reinvigorate democratic institutions, such as campaign finance reform, voting rights protections, and measures to increase civic participation. According to the Brennan Center for Justice, strengthening democratic institutions is key to maintaining a healthy democracy.

The Civic Engagement Carnival: Imagine a Civic

Engagement Carnival where the attractions are designed to educate and empower citizens. The Democratic Party can support policies that promote civic education, encourage volunteerism, and facilitate dialogue between citizens and their representatives. According to the National Conference on Citizenship, civic engagement is essential for a vibrant and responsive democracy.

The Trustworthy Town Hall: Let's host a Trustworthy Town Hall where government officials and citizens come together to share ideas and build trust. The party can advocate for regular town hall meetings, public forums, and other opportunities for direct communication between elected officials and the public. According to the Pew Research Center, open and honest communication is crucial for building trust in government.

As the Democratic Party works to address corruption, promote transparency, and restore faith in democratic institutions, it must remember that the goal is to create a government that is both effective and trustworthy. By taking steps to ensure that government serves the people with integrity and openness, the party can ensure that the American democracy is as robust and resilient as a well-built fortress.

References:

Transparency International, "Combating Corruption" (2022)
Sunlight Foundation, "Promoting Transparency" (2022)
Government Accountability Project, "Protecting Whistleblowers" (2022)

Brennan Center for Justice, "Strengthening Democratic Institutions" (2022)
National Conference on Citizenship, "Promoting Civic Engagement" (2022)
Pew Research Center, "Building Trust in Government" (2022)

Chapter 15: Media and Communication Strategies

In the grand circus of public opinion, media and communication are the ringmasters that command the spotlight. The Democratic Party has always been a performer in this circus, but in today's digital age, it's time to master the art of social media and traditional media to captivate the audience and spread the truth. Let's sprinkle some humor and a dash of digital savvy to create a communication strategy that's as engaging as a viral video and as reliable as a trusted news anchor.

Effective Use of Social Media and Traditional Media

The Social Media Spectacle: Let's turn social media into a Spectacle that's as dazzling as a fireworks display. The Democratic Party can harness the power of platforms like Twitter, Facebook, Instagram, and TikTok to connect with voters, share messages, and mobilize support. According to the Pew Research Center, social media is a primary source of news and information for many Americans, making it a crucial tool for political communication.

The Traditional Media Talent Show: Imagine a Traditional Media Talent Show where newspapers, television, and radio stations showcase their best content. The party can utilize traditional media outlets to reach a broad audience, provide in-depth analysis, and build credibility. According to the Reuters Institute for the Study of Journalism, traditional media remains influential in shaping public opinion and holding institutions accountable.

The Media Mashup: Let's create a Media Mashup that combines the immediacy of social media with the depth of traditional media. The Democratic Party can develop a comprehensive media strategy that leverages the strengths of both platforms, ensuring a balanced and effective communication approach. According to the Annenberg School for Communication, a multi-platform strategy can maximize reach and impact.

Countering Misinformation and Promoting Factual Information

The Fact-Checking Fair: Let's host a Fact-Checking Fair where misinformation is debunked and facts are celebrated. The Democratic Party can support initiatives that promote media literacy, fact-checking, and critical thinking. According to the International Fact-Checking Network, combating misinformation is essential for a healthy democracy.

The Truth Squad: Imagine a Truth Squad that patrols the information landscape, armed with facts and figures. The party can advocate for policies that support independent journalism, protect freedom of the press, and ensure that accurate information is readily available. According to the Committee to Protect Journalists, a free and independent press is vital for a well-informed public.

The Misinformation Makeover: Let's give misinformation a makeover that turns it into a paragon of truth. The Democratic Party can promote strategies that address the root causes of misinformation, such as improving education, fostering critical thinking, and building trust in reliable sources. According to the Stanford Internet Observatory, understanding and countering misinformation is a complex but necessary task.

As the Democratic Party works to effectively use social media and traditional media, and to counter misinformation and promote factual information, it must remember that the goal is to create a communication ecosystem that is both engaging and truthful. By mastering the art of media and communication, the party can ensure that its messages are as compelling and reliable as a best-selling novel.

References:

Pew Research Center, "Social Media and Political Communication" (2022)
Reuters Institute for the Study of Journalism, "The Role of Traditional Media" (2022)
Annenberg School for Communication, "Multi-Platform Media Strategy" (2022)

International Fact-Checking Network, "Combating Misinformation" (2022)
Committee to Protect Journalists, "Freedom of the Press" (2022)
Stanford Internet Observatory, "Understanding Misinformation" (2022)

Chapter 16: Grassroots Mobilization

In the grand garden of American politics, grassroots mobilization is the fertile soil that nourishes the roots of democracy. The Democratic Party has long recognized the importance of local activism, but in today's digital age, it's time to cultivate this soil with even more care and creativity. Let's sprinkle some humor and a dash of community spirit to create a grassroots movement that's as vibrant as a summer festival and as resilient as a hearty perennial.

Building Strong Local Party Structures

The Local Party Picnic: Let's throw a Local Party Picnic where everyone brings their best dish of ideas and strategies. The Democratic Party can focus on building strong local party structures by empowering local leaders, providing resources for training and development, and fostering a sense of community among members. According to the Democratic National Committee, strong local parties are the backbone of a successful national party.

The Neighborhood Networking Night: Imagine a Neighborhood Networking Night where residents of every block can meet their local party representatives and discuss issues that matter to them. The party can support policies that encourage local engagement, such as town hall meetings, community forums, and door-to-door outreach. According to the National Conference of State Legislatures, local engagement is key to understanding and addressing the needs of constituents.

The Local Leadership League: Let's create a Local Leadership League that's as competitive and fun as a community sports league. The Democratic Party can invest in programs that develop and support local leaders, providing them with the skills and confidence to take on leadership roles within the party and in their communities. According to the Leadership Conference on Civil and Human Rights, strong local leadership is essential for effective grassroots mobilization.

Engaging Volunteers and Activists at the Community Level

The Volunteer Variety Show: Let's put on a Volunteer Variety Show where every act is a different way to get involved. The Democratic Party can engage volunteers and activists by offering a variety of opportunities for participation, such as phone banking, canvassing, event planning, and social media advocacy. According to the Nonprofit Quarterly, diverse volunteer opportunities can attract and retain a broader range of supporters.

The Community Action Carnival: Imagine a Community Action Carnival where every booth is a different cause or campaign. The party can mobilize volunteers and activists by organizing events that bring together people from across the community to work on shared goals, such as voter registration drives, environmental cleanups, and food drives. According to the National Council of Nonprofits, community action builds solidarity and drives change.

The Grassroots Gratitude Gala: Let's host a Grassroots Gratitude Gala to celebrate the unsung heroes of the movement. The Democratic Party can recognize and reward volunteers and activists for their hard work and dedication, ensuring that they feel valued and motivated to continue their efforts. According to the Points of Light Foundation, recognizing volunteers is key to sustaining volunteerism and community engagement.

As the Democratic Party works to build strong local party structures and engage volunteers and activists at the community level, it must remember that the goal is to create a grassroots movement that is both inclusive and impactful. By nurturing local leadership and providing diverse opportunities for participation, the party can ensure that its grassroots efforts are as vital and enduring as a well-tended garden.

References:

Democratic National Committee, "Building Strong Local Parties" (2022) National Conference of State Legislatures, "Local Engagement and Representation" (2022) Leadership Conference on Civil and Human Rights, "Developing Local Leaders" (2022)

Nonprofit Quarterly, "Diverse Volunteer Opportunities" (2022)

National Council of Nonprofits, "Community Action and Solidarity" (2022)

Points of Light Foundation, "Recognizing Volunteers" (2022)

Chapter 17: Leadership and Vision

In the grand adventure of American politics, leadership and vision are the compass and map that guide the journey. The Democratic Party has always sought to chart a course toward a brighter future, but in today's complex world, it's time to sharpen our tools and navigate with even greater skill. Let's sprinkle some humor and a dash of inspiration to create a leadership and vision strategy that's as clear as a sunny day and as diverse as a global tapestry.

Nurturing New Leaders and Diverse Voices

The Leadership Labyrinth: Let's design a Leadership Labyrinth where emerging leaders can navigate through challenges and emerge with new skills. The Democratic Party can invest in programs that identify and develop future leaders, providing them with mentorship, training, and opportunities to gain experience. According to the Center for American Progress, nurturing new leaders is essential for the long-term health of the party and the nation.

The Diverse Voices Choir: Imagine a Diverse Voices Choir where every voice sings in harmony to create a beautiful symphony of ideas. The party can advocate for policies and practices that promote diversity and inclusion within the party's leadership ranks, ensuring that all voices are heard and valued. According to the National Democratic Institute, diverse leadership is key to representing the interests and perspectives of all Americans.

The Leadership Pipeline Project: Let's launch a Leadership Pipeline Project that's as reliable as a well-oiled machine. The Democratic Party can support initiatives that create a steady stream of new leaders, such as scholarships for political science and public administration students, internships in government offices, and leadership development programs for young professionals. According to the Aspen Institute, a robust leadership pipeline is crucial for ensuring a steady supply of talented and committed leaders.

Developing a Clear and Inspiring Vision for the Future

The Visionary Voyage: Let's embark on a Visionary Voyage where the destination is a future that's both ambitious and achievable. The Democratic Party can develop a clear and inspiring vision for the future that resonates with voters, outlining a positive and progressive agenda that addresses the challenges of today while laying the groundwork for tomorrow. According to the Brookings Institution, a compelling vision can unite supporters and drive policy initiatives.

The Future Festival: Imagine a Future Festival where the attractions are all the possibilities that lie ahead. The party can engage with voters and stakeholders to co-create a vision for the future, using workshops, town hall meetings, and online platforms to gather input and build consensus. According to the World Future Society, involving the public in visioning can lead to more innovative and inclusive outcomes.

The Inspiration Incubator:
Let's create an Inspiration Incubator where the brightest ideas for the future are hatched and nurtured. The Democratic Party can support think tanks, research institutions, and innovation hubs that focus on developing new policies and solutions for the future. According to the New America Foundation, fostering innovation is key to staying ahead of emerging challenges and opportunities.

As the Democratic Party works to nurture new leaders and diverse voices, and to develop a clear and inspiring vision for the future, it must remember that the goal is to create a movement that is both dynamic and purposeful. By investing in leadership development and crafting a vision that captures the imagination, the party can ensure that its journey is as exciting and rewarding as a treasure hunt.

References:

Center for American Progress, "Nurturing New Leaders" (2022)
National Democratic Institute, "Promoting Diverse Leadership" (2022)
Aspen Institute, "Building a Leadership Pipeline" (2022)

Brookings Institution, "Developing a Compelling Vision" (2022)
World Future Society, "Public Engagement in Visioning" (2022)
New America Foundation, "Fostering Innovation for the Future" (2022)

Chapter 18: Conclusion

In the grand finale of our political symphony, it's time to hit the high notes and bring the house down. The Democratic Party has journeyed through the chapters of reform, innovation, and vision, and now it's time to encapsulate the key points and rally the troops for the performance of a lifetime. Let's sprinkle some humor and a dash of determination to create a conclusion that's as uplifting as a standing ovation and as actionable as a to-do list.

Summary of Key Points and Actionable Steps

The Greatest Hits Album: Let's compile a Greatest Hits Album of the key points we've covered, from criminal justice reform to foreign policy, gender equality to infrastructure. The Democratic Party can use this album to remind voters of the progress we've made and the promises we've kept.

According to the Democratic National Committee, a clear and consistent message is key to electoral success.

The Actionable Steps Playbook: Imagine an Actionable Steps Playbook that's as practical as a DIY manual. The party can outline specific steps for implementing the policies and initiatives we've discussed, providing a roadmap for party members and supporters to follow. According to the Center for American Progress, actionable steps are essential for turning vision into reality.

The Progressive Agenda Planner: Let's create a Progressive Agenda Planner that's as organized as a wedding binder. The Democratic Party can develop a comprehensive agenda for the future, prioritizing issues and setting timelines for action. According to the New America Foundation, a well-planned agenda can guide the party through the complexities of governance.

Call to Action for Party Members and Supporters

The Rallying Cry: Let's issue a Rallying Cry that's as

stirring as a battle hymn. The Democratic Party can call upon its members and supporters to take action, whether it's volunteering for campaigns, advocating for policies, or simply voting in elections. According to the National Democratic Institute, grassroots action is the lifeblood of democracy.

The Volunteer Virtue: Imagine a Volunteer Virtue campaign that celebrates the everyday heroes who give their time and energy to the cause. The party can create opportunities for volunteers to get involved, from phone banking to community organizing, ensuring that every supporter has a role to play. According to the Points of Light Foundation, volunteering strengthens communities and builds social capital.

The Supporter Summit: Let's host a Supporter Summit where the party's base comes together to strategize and energize. The Democratic Party can organize events and conferences that bring together activists, donors, and elected officials to share ideas, build relationships, and plan for the future. According to the Democratic Leadership Council, unity and collaboration are essential for a strong and effective party.

As the Democratic Party concludes this journey of reinvention, it must remember that the goal is to create a movement that is both inspiring and impactful. By summarizing key points, outlining actionable steps, and calling upon party members and supporters to take action, the party can ensure that its vision for the future is as vibrant and alive as a bustling city street.

References:

Democratic National Committee, "Communicating Key Messages" (2022)
Center for American Progress, "Implementing Actionable Steps" (2022)
New America Foundation, "Planning a Progressive Agenda" (2022)
National Democratic Institute, "Grassroots Action and Democracy" (2022)

Points of Light Foundation, "Celebrating Volunteers" (2022)
Democratic Leadership Council, "Unity and Collaboration" (2022)

Drew Wohlford always had dreams of becoming a scriptwriter but then life happened. His parents divorced shortly after high school, he attended St Francis College in Fort Wayne, Indiana after wandering aimlessly in life for years. Again he found his passion for writing being encouraged by Dr. L. Carl

Nadeau, his creative writing teacher.

Then life happened again, he met his wife, Brenda. Soon there were kids and then grandkids. There were numerous jobs of all kinds, as he tried to find his passion, but it had been put on a back burner. Then in November of 2020, Drew was hit with COVID-19, which turned into long COVID and without work, and facing his 60th birthday, Drew didn't look back, he looked forward and thought, it's now or never. With a laptop in hand, he began to document the stories he told his grandchildren. The passion had once again been ignited.

Discover These Other Great Books
By Author Drew Wohlford on AMAZON

Discover These Other Great Books
By Author Drew Wohlford on AMAZON
The 4 C's for Making Diamond Employees
Drew Wohlford
Inspiration For a Pastor
Writing Obituaries For Future Generations
Twat Waffle
Drew Wohlford
Percy and the Great Boat Ride
Drew Wohlford
Drew Wohlford
Basic Multiplication Made Easy
Drew Wohlford
A Journal
Mona Lisa Has Lost Her Smile
Drew Wohlford
An Angel Named George
Drew Wohlford
VOLUME 3
Drew Wohlford
A Collection of Children's Stories
Volume 5
Drew Wohlford

Discover These Other Great Books
By Author Drew Wohlford on AMAZON
THE LENS
He got a good deal on a camera lens that might land him in prison for life.
Drew Wohlford
THE CRAIGSLIST AD
Andrew Wohlford
MADE IN CHINA
MADE IN CHINA
Drew Wohlford
HELP!
I can't figure out the best platform to write on.
Drew Wohlford
George Russo's
Best Pizza
Recipes
The secret is in the sauce
Drew Wohlford
MRS. PRESZINGLE AND THE CURIOUS TREASURE
DREW WOHLFORD
February 15th
DREW WOHLFORD
DEARLY DEMENTED
Drew Wohlford
ODBODY
The Humble Clockmaker
Drew Wohlford
Breakfast On The Beach
365 Devotionals to get closer to Jesus
Drew Wohlford
Like A Country Song
Drew Wohlford
Bodies In The Backyard
My First 60 Years
Drew Wohlford
An Autobiography

Discover These Other Great Books
By Author Drew Wohlford on AMAZON

Discover These Other Great Books
By Author Drew Wohlford on AMAZON
Charm School
of hard knocks
Drew Wohlford
Loretta Johnson
AND THE CASE
OF THE WIPED
OUT SNOWDUDE
Drew Wohlford

Switched
Drew Wohlford
Peroloco Publishing
My Neighbor Charged Her car !
(A look at America's Electric
Infrastucture and Electric cars)
Drew Wohlford
"SELF" HELP
There Is No Such Thing
Drew Wohlford

Who Left The Ladder Of Success in the Middle of My Failure?
A look at success and failure with a little humor
Drew Wohlford
DEMENTIA
Killer Dolphin
DREW WOHLFORD
Breakfast On The Beach
365 Short Devotionals for everyday life
DREW WOHLFORD
Outside The Bedroom
(How to really love a woman)
Drew Wohlford

Farmer Bob
and the very
big garden
Drew Wohlford

"Not all angels you encounter are
good, some are very, very bad".
D'Pressions Bar and Grill
Drew Wohlford

Octowolf
Drew Wohlford

WE LIVE IN
HELL
Drew Wohlford

IN THE BASEMENT
THE CONTINUING ADVENTURES OF
THE HOODED VULTURE AND MEERKAT
#6
Drew Wohlford
HAIRY MAN
DREW WOHLFORD
Lost In Time
"Harry was a genius. We studied computer science together, and he always talked about creating something revolutionary. When he first told me about ChronoLeap, I thought he was crazy. Time travel? It sounded like science fiction"
Drew Wohlford
THE FALL OF DOCTOR CARNEY
DREW WOHLFORD

A Collection Of Children's Stories
Volume 8
Drew Wohlford
Guest Authors
Sarah Wohlford- Moysin
Mikayla Carr

The Blood Of Wolfordville
Drew Wohlford

The Literary Marketing Odyssey
How To Market Your Book For Free
365 Days Of Blessings
Breakfast On The Beach
Drew Wohlford
DREW WOHLFORD

Clara and the Dairy Cow Isopods
Drew Wohlford

www.ingramcontent.com/pod-product-compliance
Lightning Source LLC
Chambersburg PA
CBHW061345250726

48657CB00004B/1332